Copyright

The rights of all texts contained in this electronic book are reserved to its author, and are registered and protected by copyright laws. This is an electronic edition (ebook), which cannot be sold or marketed under any circumstances, nor used for any purposes involving monetary interest.

The archetypes in marketing

Archetypes in marketing emerged from the theory of archetypes by Carl Jung, a Swiss psychologist who developed a theory that describes the deep motivations and common behavior patterns that affect human consciousness.

Jung argued that archetypes are unconscious motivators that influence human behavior.

He believed that these archetypes are rooted deep within the human psyche and are responsible for creating recurring attitudes and behaviors.

This theory was later applied to marketing in order to create advertisements that connect with people's deep motivations and needs.

In marketing, archetypes are used to create an image or brand that connects with the deep feelings and emotions that people have when thinking about certain products or services.

According to Jung, there are 12 types of existing archetypes:

the innocent;
the wise man;
the hero;
the rebel;
the explorer;
the magician;

the common person;

the lover;

the fool;

the caregiver;

the creator;

the ruler;

This image summarizes well where each of the 12 archetypes are:

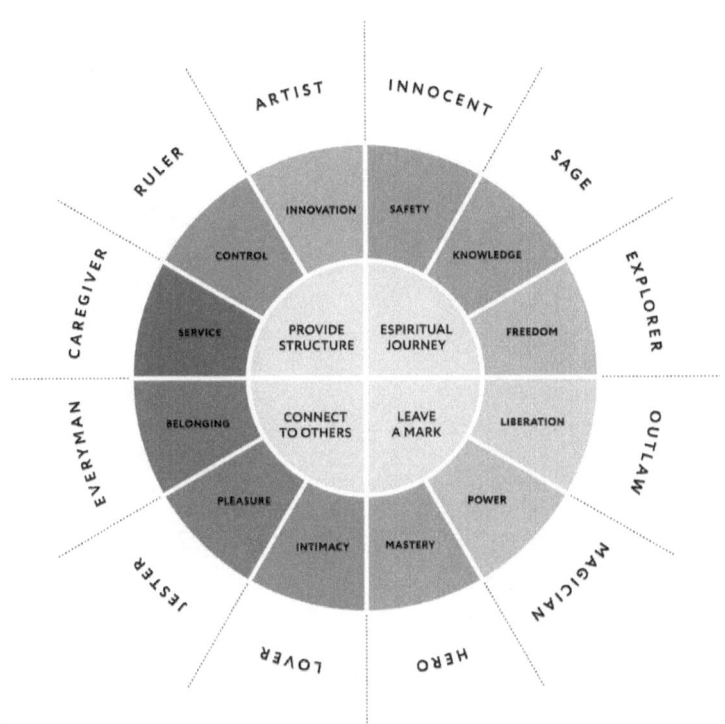

Now, you will get to know each one of them and learn how to use them in your brand.

Good reading!

THE INNOCENT

The archetype of the innocent is the one who is seen as having a pure and naive heart. They are remembered as those who believe that everyone is good and that the world is a wonderful place. They present themselves as being the most innocent and trustworthy of all.

They are generally seen as those who have a deep love for life and the people around them, always ready to help and serve. They are loyal, compassionate, kind and generous, wanting to help others, even if it means losing something in return.

The innocent archetype also believes that the worldit's full of possibilities, and that it is possible to achieve anything.

They are not afraid to dream and pursue their dreams. They believe that life is meant to be lived, not just lived in the mind.

The innocent archetype can often be seen as naive and ungrateful. Remembered for their faith, determination and hope, they believe that all problems have solutions, and that everything will work out in the end.

In the end, the innocent archetype feels that life is to be lived in joy, hope, and peace.

Its features are:

- Faith
- determination
- hope
- generosity
- loyalty
- trust
- love
- kindness
- naive
- kindness
- generosity
- innocence.

A great example of someone who is known for his innocent archetype is actor and comedian Robin Williams.

He is known for his way of looking at life in a cheerful, fun and optimistic way.

He is a great defender of human rights, always ready to help those in need.

He also stands out for his kind and gentle way of treating people, making everyone around him feel good. Robin Williams is famous for his funny and innocent side, which makes him always comment on life and matters in general in an entertaining way.

But how can I adapt this archetype to my brand?

To implement the innocent archetype in an Instagram ad, for example, use a warm, kind and generous approach.

A good way to do this is to show an image of a person who is smiling and having fun, and use copy (text) that highlights the kindness, optimism and hope that the innocent archetype brings to the world.

For example, the copy could say something like:

"The worldit's full of possibilities when you believe that everything will work out in the end". This would help communicate the message and bring out the archetype of the innocent".

THE WISE MAN

The archetype of the sage is one who is seen as having the ability to look beyond conventional perspectives and see the truth behind appearances.

They are remembered as those who believed that wisdom comes from within and that wisdom manifests itself in the decisions we make.

are usually seen as those who have a deep knowledge and understanding of life, and who can use that knowledge to help others.

They are wise, intuitive, patient and understanding. They want to help us learn and teach us how to make the right choices.

The sage archetype is also believed that knowledge comes from experiences and that wisdom is something that is acquired over time.

Finally, the sage archetype shows that wisdom comes from within and that life's experiences teach us to live happier and more fulfilled. With an open mind to understand the world around us, he shows us how we are able to find wisdom within ourselves.

Its main features are:

- Wisdom
- intuition
- patience
- understanding
- knowledge
- experience
- true understanding
- discernment

A prime example of someone who is known for his sage archetype is spiritual leader and philosopher Deepak Chopra.

His career is filled with contributions to the understanding of life, the universe and human existence.

He is known for his deep knowledge and understanding of life, as well as his intuitive wisdom.

Chopra is a great advocate of knowledge and understanding of life, always concerned with helping people understand the universe.

He stands out for his patience, understanding and ability to see the truth behind appearances.

Adapting this archetype for digital marketing, I would use a welcoming, intuitive and realistic approach.

A good way to do this is to show an image of someone who is meditating and reflective, and use copy that highlights the wisdom, intuition, and truth that the sage archetype brings to the world.

For example, the copy could say something like:

"Wisdom comes from within and teaches us to find the truth behind appearances".

This would help communicate the message and bring out the archetype of the sage.

Other examples like:

"Wisdom is the key to discovering the meaning of life."

"Do not let appearancesdeceive, look for the truth".

Realize that the big idea is to use your own characteristics to create the texts.

THE HERO

The hero archetype stands out for its courage, strength, determination and bravery.

They are known to be those who are always ready to face challenges and fight for justice. They are always willing to sacrifice everything for the greater good of all.

They fight against dark and evil forces, and are always ready to do whatever it takes to save the day.

They aren't afraid to risk their own lives to save others, and they're willing to do what's right.

The hero archetype does not give up, no matter what. They are remembered for their persistence and will to win, and for their positive and optimistic side.

Despite all adversity, they know they can improve the world.

In the end, the hero archetype is one who believes that nothing is impossible.

Its characteristics are:

- Courage
- strength
- determination
- bravura
- persistence
- optimism
- heroism
- sacrifice
- justice.

A character that utilizes the hero archetype is Marvel's Captain America.

Known for his courage, strength and bravery, and for his determination to save the world.

He is the protector of the weak and the oppressed, and is always ready to fight evil forces.

Captain America is also known for his persistence and his will to win, and for his positive and optimistic side. He believes that it is possible to change the world for the better, despite all the adversities.

For a persuasive ad with the hero archetype, use a gritty, gritty approach.

A good way to do this is to show a picture of an ordinary person doing something heroically noble.

For example, the image could show a person helping another person in need. The copy could say something like:

"You don't need superpowers to help someone."

This would help communicate the message and bring out the hero archetype.

An example of a Nike ad that highlighted the hero archetype was its 2016 campaign titled "Unlimited".

The ad highlighted the notion that we all have the potential to be heroes.

The ad copy read, "There are no limits to what you can achieve. Be the hero the world needs."

The campaign was a success and highlighted the hero archetype in a unique and effective way.

THE REBEL

The rebel archetype is one who is always ready to challenge the rules and question authority. They are remembered as those who believed that the rules should be challenged and that true freedom must be won.

They believe that laws should be questioned and that people should have the right to express their own opinions.

They are generally seen as having a deep sense of justice and a desire to change the world.

They are loyal, determined and courageous, willing to fight for those who have no voice.

They believe that laws and rules should protect and not control.

The archetype of the rebel is also the one who believes that true freedom is only achieved through action. They are not afraid to question and challenge the rules, and they are ready to face the consequences.

In the end, the rebel archetype comes from action, not passivity, and that change is only achieved in conflict.

Its characteristics are:

- Determination
- courage
- justice
- loyalty
- rebellion
- freedom
- questioning

- action
- challenge
- independence.

In the movie The Matrix, Neo is one of the main characters who uses the outlaw archetype.

Throughout the film, he is seen as one who defies rules and authorities, such as the Matrix.

He proves to be determined, courageous and loyal to his goal of freeing humanity from the Matrix's rule.

Use your sense of justice to fight the Matrix's rules and authorities and save those in need.

In the end, he ends up managing to free humanity from the Matrix's domain, showing that true freedom comes from action and not from passivity.

Moving to the marketing side now, one of the most famous Harley-Davidson ads that uses the outlaw archetype is the "Live to Ride" ad.

The ad shows a character defying the laws of nature and authorities, riding a Harley-Davidson through challenging terrain.

The copy highlights the strength, courage and determination that the outlaw archetype brings.

This ad helped communicate the message and bring out the outlaw archetype.

To adapt the outlaw archetype to your brand, use an approach that highlights the determination, courage, and justice that the outlaw archetype brings.

A good way to do this is to use an image that shows a character defying rules and authority.

THE EXPLORER

The Explorer archetype is one who loves to push his limits and venture into new territories.

They are always looking for new experiences and new discoveries, and they are not afraid to step out of their comfort zone to explore the world.

They are seen as those who have a deep love for liberty and free speech.

They are loyal, courageous and determined, and fear nothing. They are always ready to take risks and venture into new conquests.

They also believe that all the answers are out there in the world, and that it is through searching for those answers that they will discover what they really want.

They are ambitious, creative and always willing to learn new skills.

Remembered for their willingness to take risks and venture out in search of new discoveries.

In the end, the explorer archetype is one who believes that life is to be lived with curiosity, joy and courage.

Its main features are:

- freedom;
- mundane;
- outgoing;
- adventurous;
- brave;
- in love with the world.

Indiana Jones is a great example of the explorer archetype.

Known for his way of facing life in an adventurous and audacious way, always in search of new discoveries and adventures.

In addition, he is known for his curious and creative side, which makes him always explore new paths and learn new skills.

Heineken used the explorer archetype very well in its ads and quite rightly.

They used an adventurous, courageous and creative approach. They showed images of people who were ready to go on an adventure, and used copy that highlighted the freedom, optimism, and curiosity that the explorer archetype brings to the world.

For example, if you adapt the copy for your brand, you could say something like:

"Be an explorer, and discover what's beyond the limits".

This would bring out the explorer archetype.

THE MAGICIAN

The wizard archetype is seen as a symbol of wisdom and power.

They are remembered for having a deep knowledge and understanding of the nature of reality.

They present themselves as being the wisest and most gifted of all.

Generally seen as those who have the ability to see the mysteries of the world and the truth that is beyond what we can perceive.

They are loyal, intelligent, creative and self-assured, willing to share their knowledge with others, even if it means losing something in return.

The magician archetype is also the one who believes to achieve anything with the power of the mind and the ability to see the world differently.

Nohe has afraid to think and create.

They can often be seen as mystics and intellectuals.

In the end, the wizard archetype believes that the world is full of possibilities, and that life is meant to be lived with wisdom, creativity, and power.

Its main features are:
- Mysticism
- intuition
- creativity
- intelligence
- loyalty

- security
- knowledge
- can
- intellectuality
- understanding
- ability.

Using the Dr. Strange as an example, he is known as the archetype of the mage, the character was built to portray that.

He is a brilliant and successful doctor, but who, after an accident, discovers that there is a mysterious world beyond what is visible. He then embarks on a journey to learn and gain knowledge to save the world.

During his journey, he discovers that he has mystical powers, and that he is able to manipulate reality. He also discovers that his ability to think creatively and intuitively is his greatest weapon.

The character of Dr. Strange was built to showcase the strength and wisdom we all possess to face life's challenges. He is a symbol of knowledge.

Let's look at how Red Bull used the wizard archetype in a marketing campaign.

The ad featured a mysterious, hooded man who was capable of great feats.

The man performed amazing skills such as drawing a cartoon and creating music.

At the end of the ad, the man reveals that he is the Magician and is able to accomplish these things because he drinks Red Bull.

The ad uses the wizard archetype to show that Red Bull is the powerhouse for those looking to achieve great things.

THE ORDINARY PERSON

The common person archetype is one of the oldest archetypes created by Carl Jung.

It was created as a way to express what is common to all human beings, regardless of their cultural, religious or social differences.

It is formed by a common set of characteristics, qualities and behaviors that all human beings, in general, possess.

This includes traits such as honesty, loyalty, generosity, kindness, hope, and faith.

These traits are as old as mankind and have been passed down from generation to generation.

Furthermore, these traits are also important for self-development as they help us to preserve our individuality and find our way in life.

The archetype of the average person is one of the main archetypes in our society, which is why it is so important to us.

It is through the awareness of the existence of this archetype that we can connect with others and create healthy and lasting relationships.

Bill Gates is a classic example of the everyman archetype. He was born in 1955, in Seattle, United States, and from an early age showed his talent for technology.

He went to study at Harvard University, but ended up leaving his studies to follow his dream of creating a technology company.

He founded Microsoft at the age of 20 and was one of the pioneers in creating an operating system for computers. It made Microsoft one of the biggest companies in the world, and today Microsoft is considered one of the biggest companies in the world.

In addition to his business success, Bill Gates is also known for his humanitarian side. He dedicated part of his fortune to helping those in need, in addition to funding charitable projects and scientific research.

Known for his generosity and dedication to others, characteristics that are common to the common person archetype.

Bill Gates is an example that it is possible to achieve success ethically and honestly, and he is also an example that it is possible to use success to help those in need.

Definitely a great example of the everyman archetype.

Now, see an example of the Hering brand.

One marketing campaign that Hering used to highlight the archetype of the common man was the campaign "The Power of Clothing", which was launched in 2017.

The campaign showed a group of men dressed in Hering clothes, showing that clothes can help reflect who we are and what we want for our lives.

It showed a variety of men, with different ages, nationalities, professions and lifestyles, all wearing Hering clothes.

The campaign highlighted that Hering clothes symbolize the common man's power to achieve his goals and dreams.

THE LOVER

The Lover archetype is one of the most ancient and well-known human archetypes, being one of the main motifs of art and literature since ancient times.

It is the one who is seen as the one who is willing to sacrifice everything to help those he loves.

They are remembered for having a deep love for life, family and those around them.

Loyal, compassionate, kind and generous, wanting to help others even if it means losing something in return.

They are strong defenders of their ideals and believe that love is the greatest force in the world.

Over the centuries, the Lover archetype has evolved to adapt to changes in its culture and the modern world, but its core values remain the same.

They are firm believers in love and self-sacrifice to help others. Love is the most powerful force and it is the only cure for any problem.

They can often be seen as altruistic. Remembered for their faith, determination and hope. In the end, the Lover archetype believes that love is the greatest force in the world, and that great things can be accomplished with love and companionship.

Carrying the archetype into the story, Romeo was a passionate young man living in Verona.

He was known for his great love and kindness, and his desire to help those around him.

He had a deep love for his beloved, Juliet, and would do anything to show his love for her.

Juliet's father once forbade Romeo to see his daughter, but he didn't let that stop him from his love.

Instead, he went to find Juliet and they both decided to run away together. Romeo put aside all his plans so that he and Juliet could run away together.

Romeo risked his life to save his beloved, and ended up finding death so they could be together. He sacrificed himself to save Juliet's life and showed his deep love for her.

The Lover archetype is symbolized by Romeo, who went out of his way to show his love and companionship to Juliet.

THE FOOL

The jester archetype is a character type that was created thousands of years ago as part of ancient culture.

He is characterized as that person who is foolish and naive, but who is still adored and loved by everyone.

Created to serve as a form of comic relief for people, he is seen as that figure who always means well, but still ends up making mistakes and saying the wrong things.

The jester is also remembered as the one who is always ready to help, and who has a pure and kind heart.

The silly archetype is still used to this day in various media such as movies, cartoons, and television shows.

Often used to create funny and amusing scenes, and to help tell the story. Used as a way to promote kindness and generosity in the midst of life's chaos and difficulties.

The silly archetype is a character who continues to be loved and adored by everyone to this day, and who helps bring a little light and joy into the world. It is still used to teach valuable lessons to inspire people to be more compassionate and kind to those around them.

A classic example is Homer Simpson who is the main character of the cartoon series The Simpsons.

He was created with the aim of becoming the silly archetype of the series. Characterized as an ordinary, hard-working man who has a tendency to make mistakes and say the wrong things.

Homer is remembered as that figure who has good intentions, but who gets involved in funny and fun adventures. Also known for his kind and loving heart which always drives him to help those around him and to do whatever he can to help.

Despite his silliness, Homer is adored and teaches everyone that it is possible to find joy and happiness even in the midst of life's difficulty and chaos.

His silly archetype still inspires people.

To adapt your brand to the archetype, use an approach that highlights the kindness, optimism and joy that the jester brings to the world.

A good way to do this is to use an image of a person who is smiling and having fun, and use copy that highlights the comedy.

THE CAREGIVER

The caregiver archetype is one who is always willing to help others. They are compassionate, kind, and dedicated to caring for others.

This archetype is always willing to embrace those in need of love and attention, and they are willing to do whatever it takes to help those they love.

Caregivers are often loyal and protective, and they strive to provide security and stability. They also have a great sense of responsibility and are devoted to the people they love.

It is a type of figure that is often portrayed in movies and books.

In marketing, the caregiver archetype is used to create an image or brand that connects with people's need to feel loved and protected. In advertisements, the caregiver archetype is used to highlight the importance of family and community, and how important it is to care for each other.

Let's use Gandalf from Lord of the Rings as an example.

Gandalf uses the caretaker archetype to build the narrative.

He is a wise and experienced character who helps guide and protect Frodo and the other party members.

Gandalf is seen as a protective, compassionate and loyal figure, making him an ideal caregiver archetype.

He is always looking to think of everyone's welfare, not just Frodo's.

He is represented as a character who is able to offer advice and guidance to the group, which is a typical feature of the archetype.

It also highlights the important role of family and community in history. It shows that even in times of great danger and despair, those who care about the well-being of others are able to offer the love and support that is essential to everyone's success.

A good way to use the caregiver archetype in Instagram ads is to show the impact on people's lives. That means showing how the product or service is helping people live healthier, safer, happier and more productive lives.

Highlight the importance of community and family. For example, showing how the product or service is helping to connect people and making them feel loved and protected.

One of the most famous ads depicting the caregiver archetype is Apple's television ad for the iPhone X.

The ad tells the story of a mother and her son who use the iPhone to stay in touch and connect.

Throughout the ad, we see how the mother uses the iPhone to accompany her son in his day-to-day activities. She also uses her iPhone to keep him connected while he's at school, and to keep him safe when he's having fun.

The ad highlights the mother's protective and compassionate role, and her unconditional love for her child. Plus, it shows how essential the iPhone is to connecting people and caring for the ones we love.

THE CREATOR

The creator archetype is one of the main ones that motivate human behavior. It represents people's creative ability, as well as the desire to create something new.

It is a very versatile archetype as it encompasses all types of creation, from creating works of art and music to creating innovative products.

To help explore the creator archetype, it's important to understand what motivates you. The creator is motivated by creativity, curiosity and innovation.

He has a deep desire to discover new things and create something unique and innovative.

He also has a deep desire for the freedom to be creative and express his ideas.

In marketing, the creator archetype can be used to motivate people to try something new. For example, companies can use advertisements to highlight the benefits of trying something new, such as a new product or service. This approach can help create a sense of discovery and creativity for people, encouraging them to take action.

An example was Henry Ford, one of the first to use the creator archetype in his story.
He used this archetype to highlight his creative and innovative spirit, as well as his desire to create something new.

Ford pioneered affordable cars for the general public.

He believed that everyone should have access to cars and that they should be built affordably.

It created the assembly line that would be used to build cars faster and cheaper, making them accessible to the general public.

In marketing, Ford used the creator archetype to highlight his product's innovation and curiosity.

He also used the archetype to emphasize his desire for freedom. He believed that everyone should have the right to drive a car. That's what motivated him to create the assembly line, as he knew it would allow more people to have access to cars.

So Henry Ford used these elements to create an affordable product that would allow more people to have access to cars.

In the end, by using the creator archetype in your marketing strategy, you can help people see what's possible when they allow themselves to be creative.

THE GOVERNOR

The ruler archetype describes the personality of someone who is naturally leader, responsible and authoritative.

This personality usually has an intuitive and decisive nature.

They are extremely results-oriented and tend to play leadership and responsibility roles. Motivated by results and always want to be recognized for their work and success.

In marketing, the ruler archetype is used to attract people who tend to connect with natural leaders. Ads using the ruler archetype usually show someone in a leadership role, making important decisions and being accountable for results. This approach can help build a sense of trust, which can help increase sales.

Marvel Comics used the ruler archetype to create the narrative for their superhero Thor.

Thor was the God of Thunder and son of the God Odin, King of Asgard.

He showed his strength and leadership by defeating his enemies and protecting the weak.

Also, he was known for his great courage and determination.

Marvel used this ruler archetype when creating the narrative as a responsible and leading character.

Some Marvel ads show Thor battling his enemies and touching readers' hearts. This helped build a sense of confidence and authority around the character, which helped increase sales.

To adapt this archetype to your brand, you can build image or video ads that show a person making important decisions or leading others. This will help reinforce the message of leadership and accountability.

USING MULTIPLE LAYERS OF ARCHETYPES

Archetypes are used to create a narrative for the brand, so if you want to create a multi-layered character, you can use multiple archetypes. However, it's important to remember that using too many archetypes can be counterproductive, as it can make the character too complex and difficult to understand.

Ideally, choose archetypes that work together and are consistent with the message you want to convey.

After choosing the archetypes, it is necessary to develop the characteristics of the character according to each one.

This includes the character's personality, goals, motivations, challenges, and abilities.

You can also create a character backstory to bring your archetype to life.

Finally, remember that each archetype should complement each other and be consistent with the message you want to convey.

COMBINING THE ARCHETYPES

The best way to combine archetypes to create a character for your brand is to think about the message you want to convey.

Consider which traits and qualities you want to highlight, then choose the archetypes that best fit that message.

It's also important to consider your brand's target audience and choose archetypes that connect with them.

For example, if your target audience is young people, you can use the Explorer or Hero archetype to create a character that connects with that age group.

Try to create a character that is authentic, unique and memorable, but consistent with your brand values, mission and vision.

See some examples:

Hero and Explorer: This combination reflects the hero's quest for challenge and determination, combined with the explorer's curiosity and adventure.

Sage and Mage: This combination represents the wisdom of the sage combined with the ability to manipulate the world around the mage.

Innocent and Caregiver: This combination represents innocence combined with caretaker concern and compassion.

Rebel and Lover: This combination reflects the independence and free spirit of the rebel, combined with the affection of the lover.

Creator and Ordinary Person: This combination reflects the creativity of the creator, combined with the simplicity and practicality of the common person.

Jester and Ruler: Reflects the naivety of the jester, combined with the authority and responsibility of the ruler.

By combining archetypes in pairs, it is possible to create rich and interesting characters that can be used to create strong and memorable brands. Using archetypes to create characters can also help marketers create engaging stories and narratives that can connect with target audiences. If you're looking for a way to create strong characters and memorable brands, using archetypes is an excellent option.

CONCLUSION

This book offers a unique approach to creating persuasive marketing ads.

He explains the 12 personality archetypes that can be used to create more effective marketing ads.

The strategies in this book allow people to understand consumer behavior and create ads that specifically target them.

With a simple approach from this book, you will have more attractive advertisements and thus achieve your desired marketing objectives.

It's a must-read for any professional who wants to create effective ads and attract more consumers.

Who is Matheus Martins Soares?

Matheus is an Ex-Military / Presidential Agent, graduated in Marketing since 2018 and specialist in copywriting. He has written for more than 27 different niches, showing his ability to adapt to different topics and audiences. Throughout his career, he has worked in large companies, such as the largest business magazine in the country and the largest marketing consultancy in Brazil. Contributed to the success of important campaigns, generating + 30mm in sales for its customers. Published over 100 books on Amazon and gained readers in over 10 different countries. An expert in StoryTelling and UX Writing, he also works behind the scenes as a GhostWriter, giving voice to other people's ideas and stories. His method is capable of writing a book in less than 24 hours.

With a strategic vision and knowledge in marketing, he helps companies, authors and literary projects to achieve success. He found himself in the world of marketing, writing and human behavior, his ability to adapt to different challenges is a differential that makes him stand out in his field.